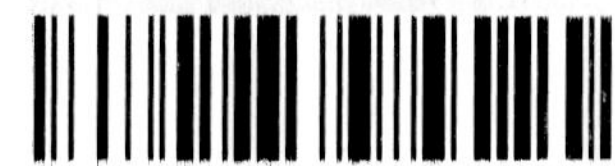

START WITH BISMILLAH

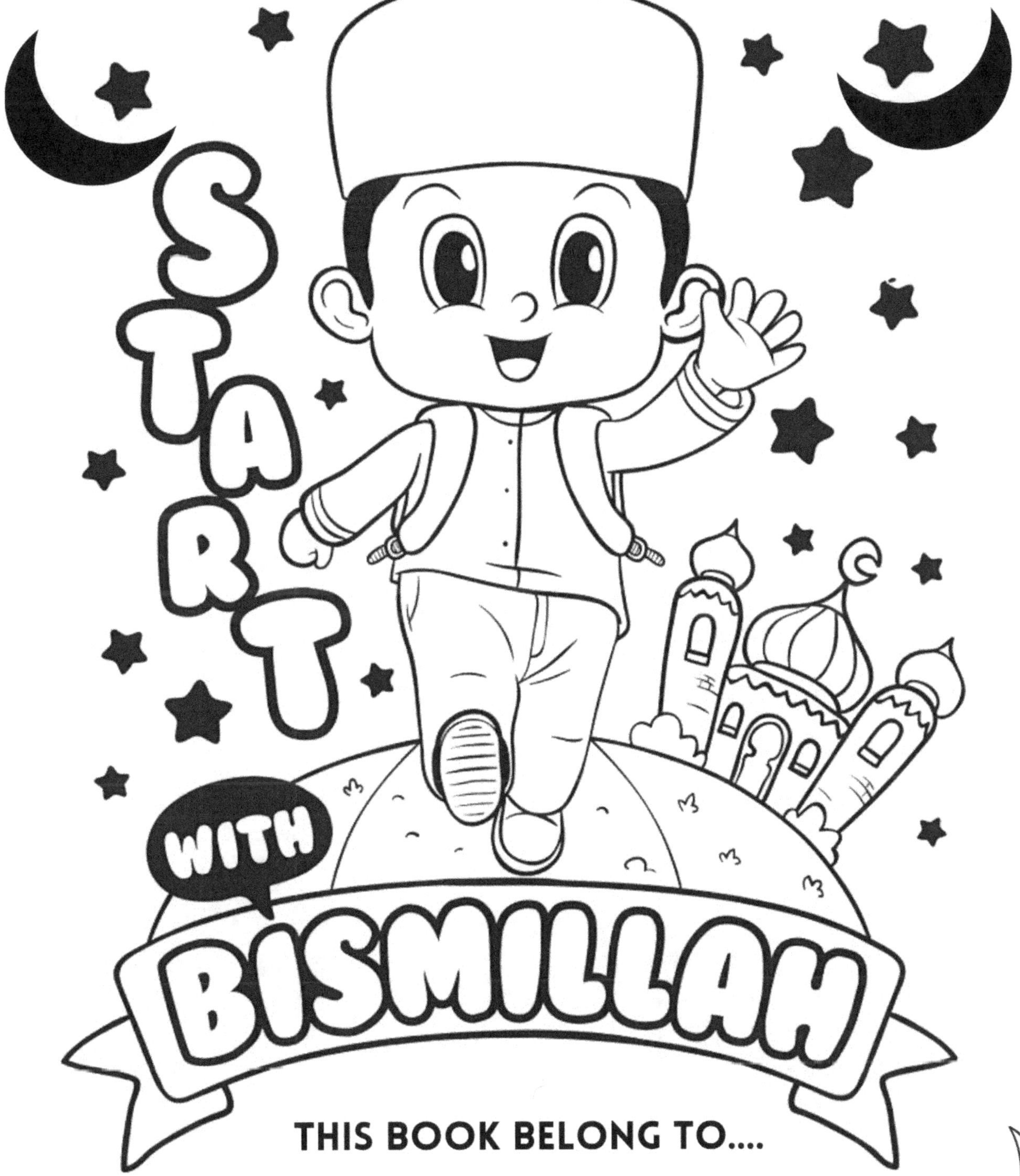

THIS BOOK BELONG TO....

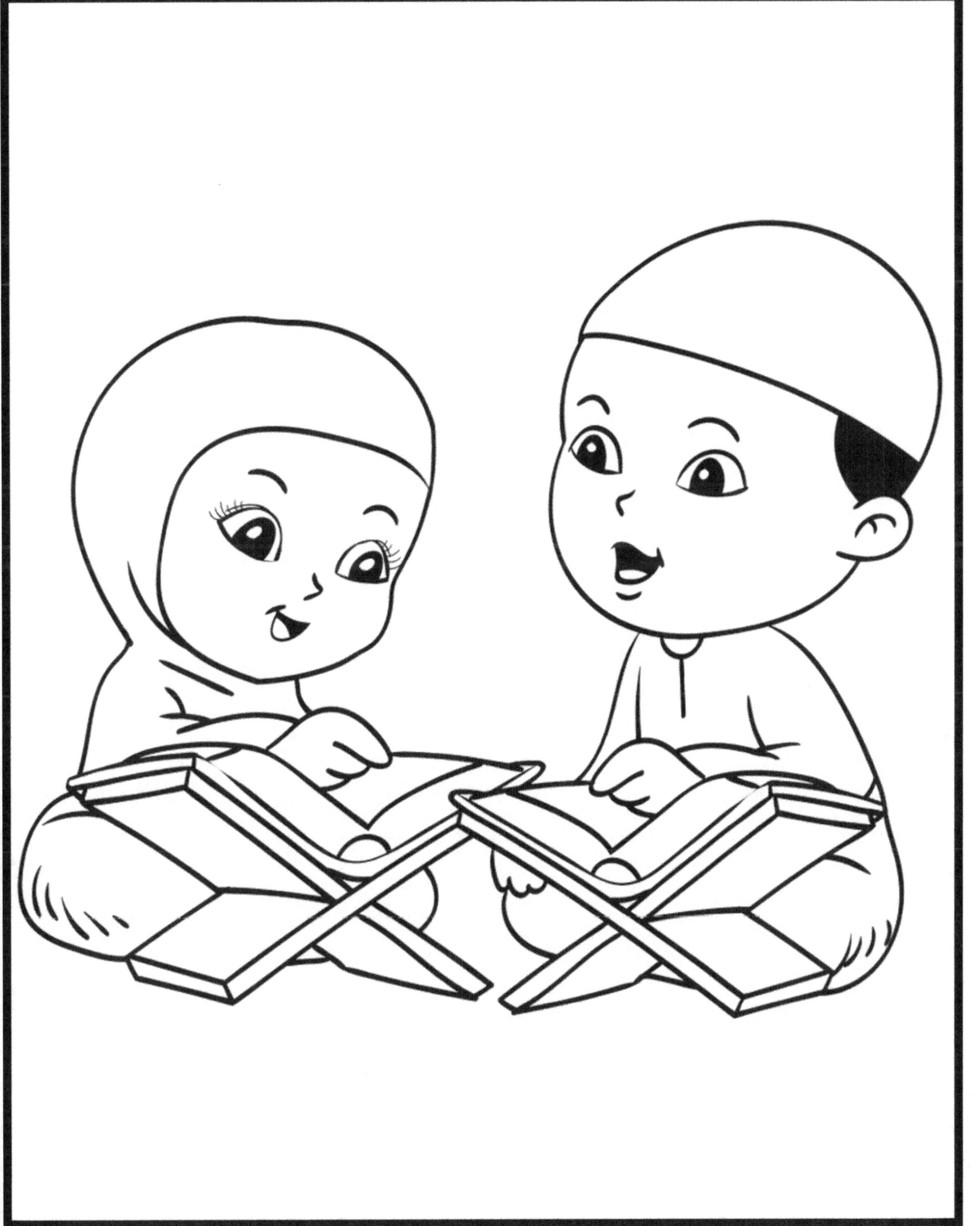

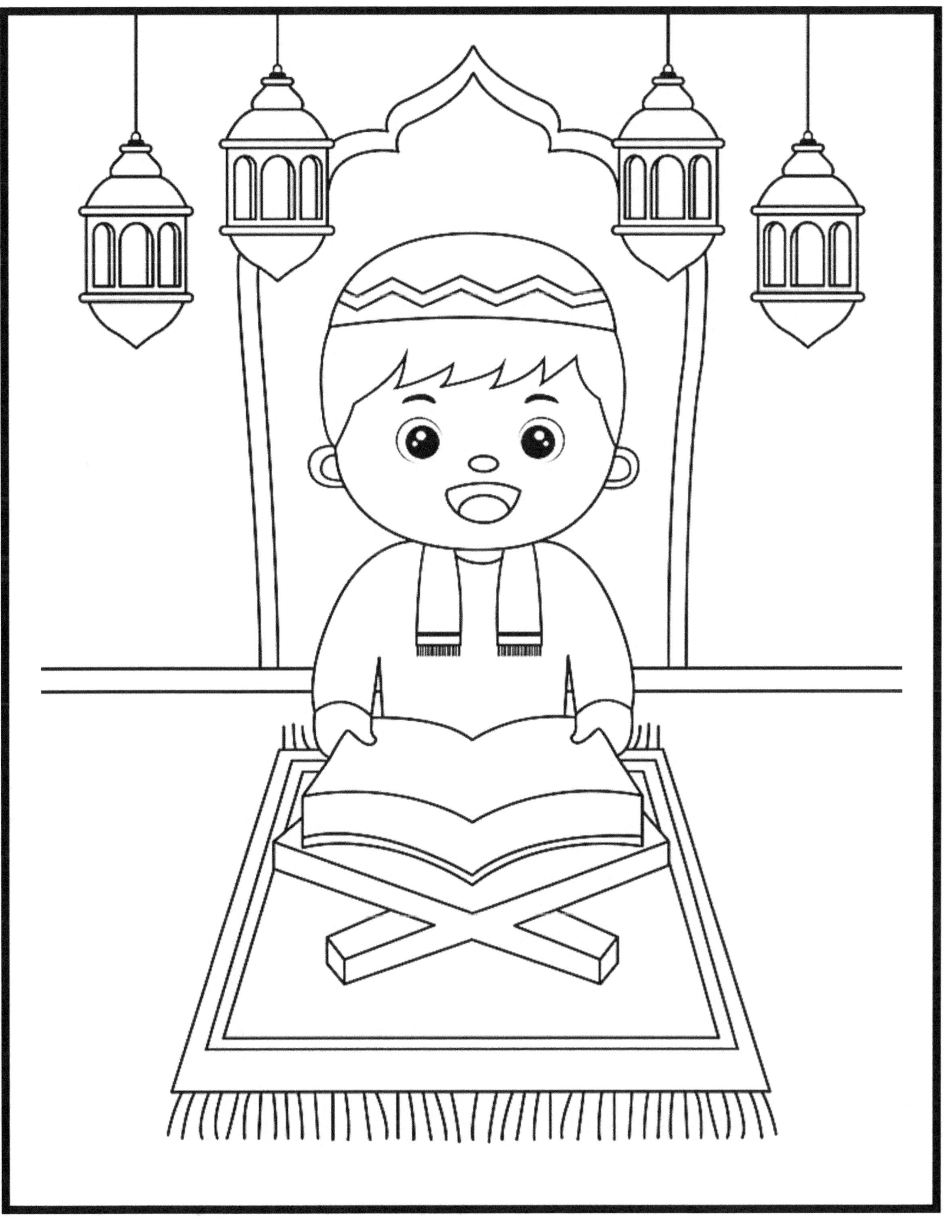

Iftar

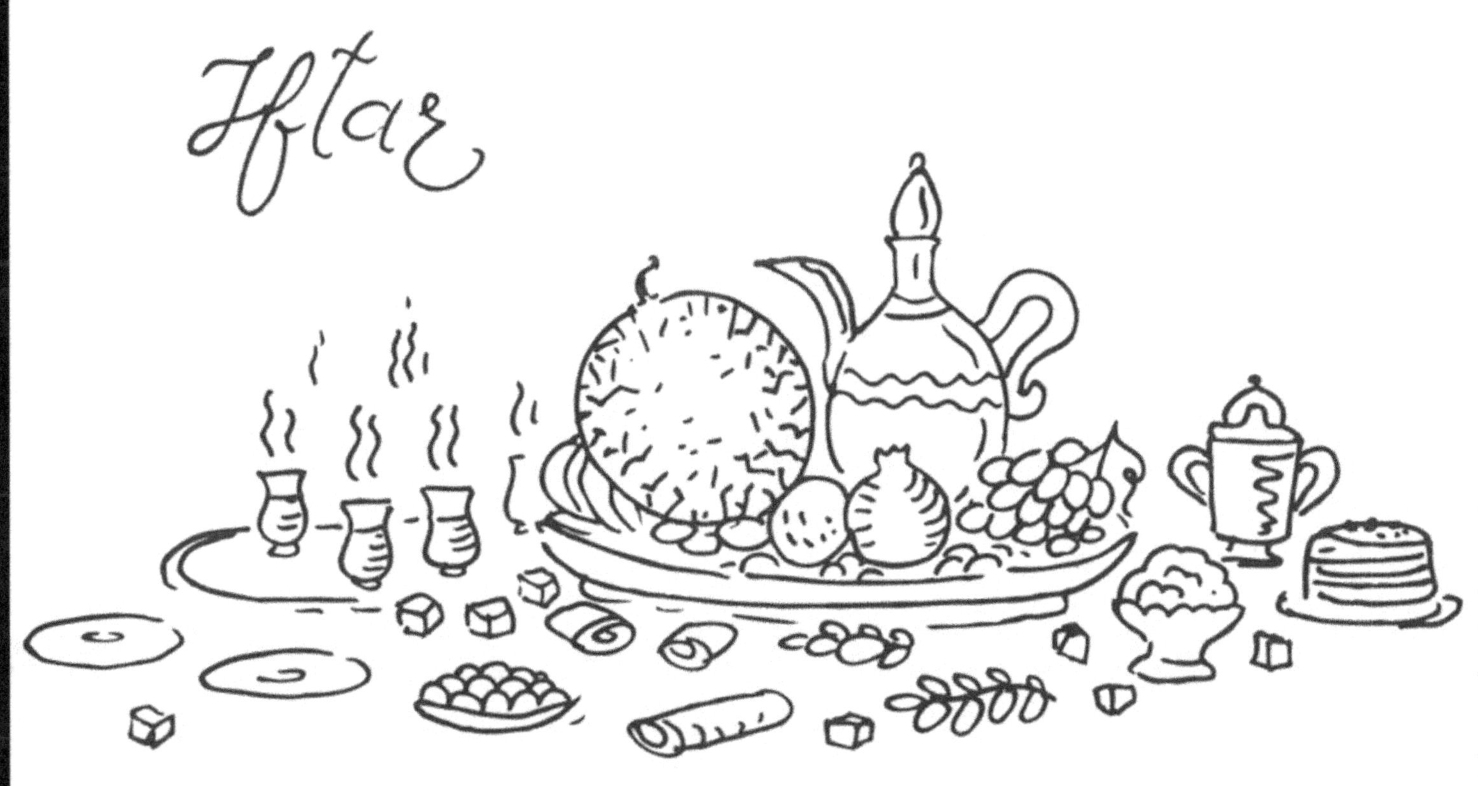

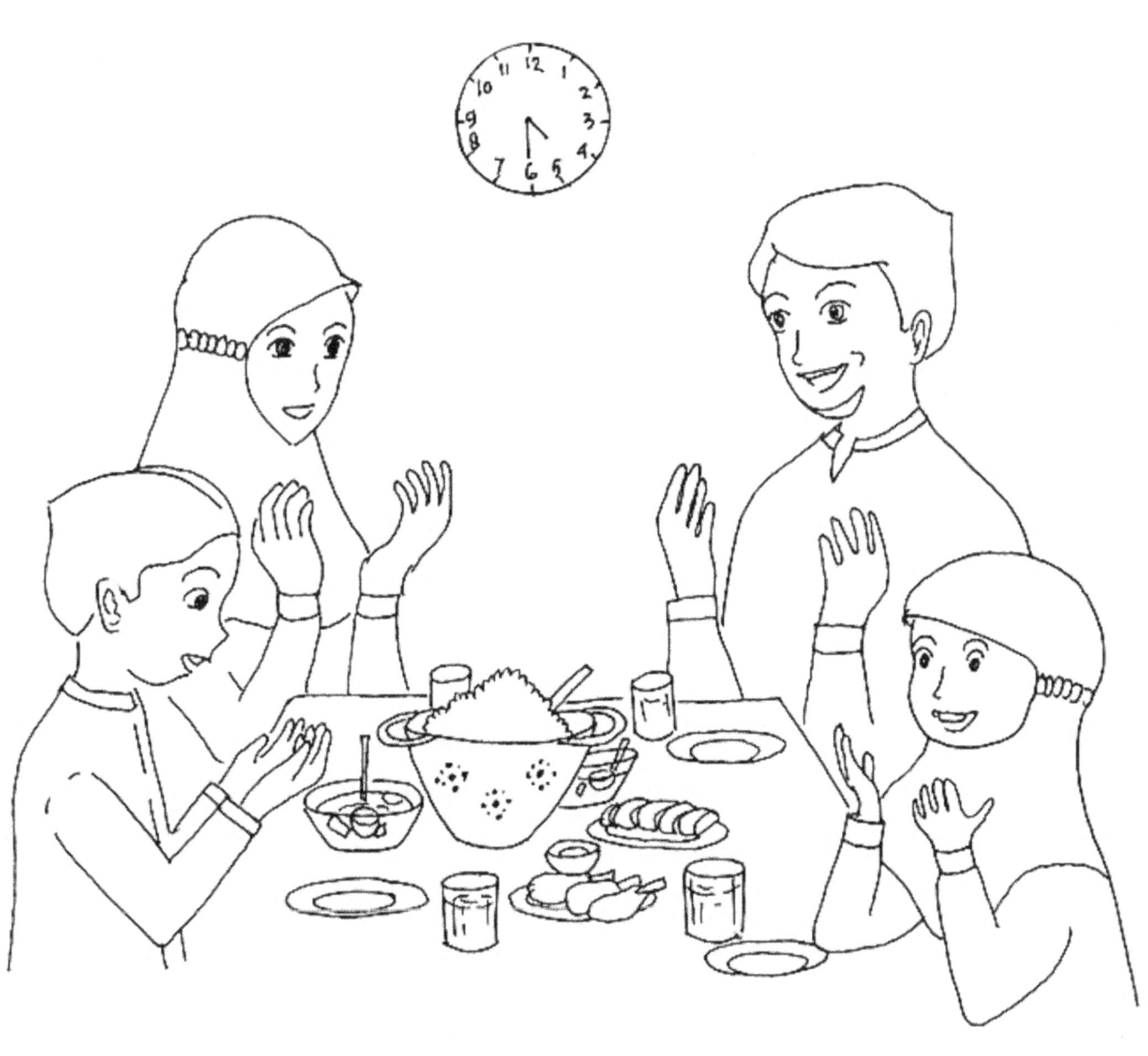

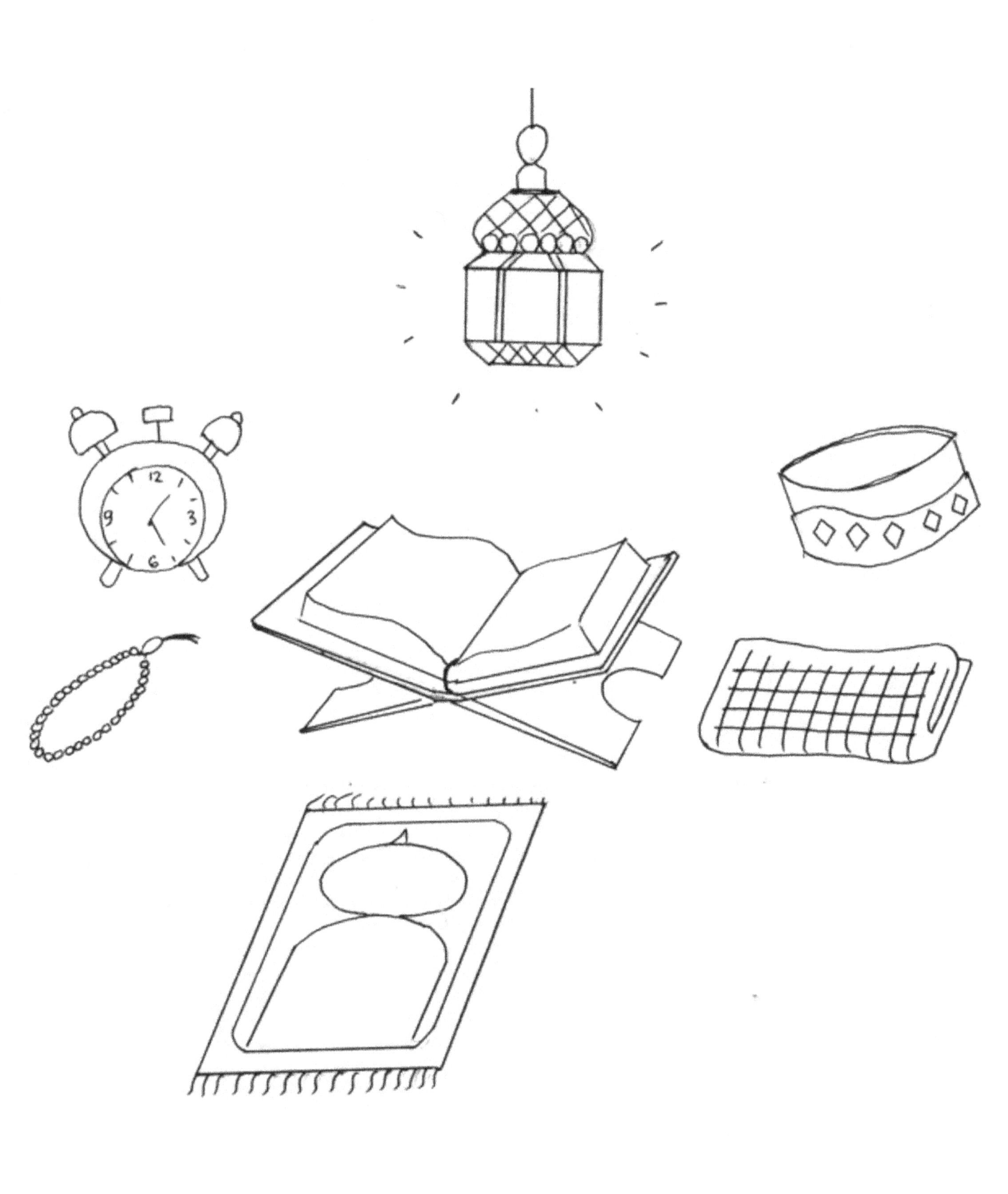

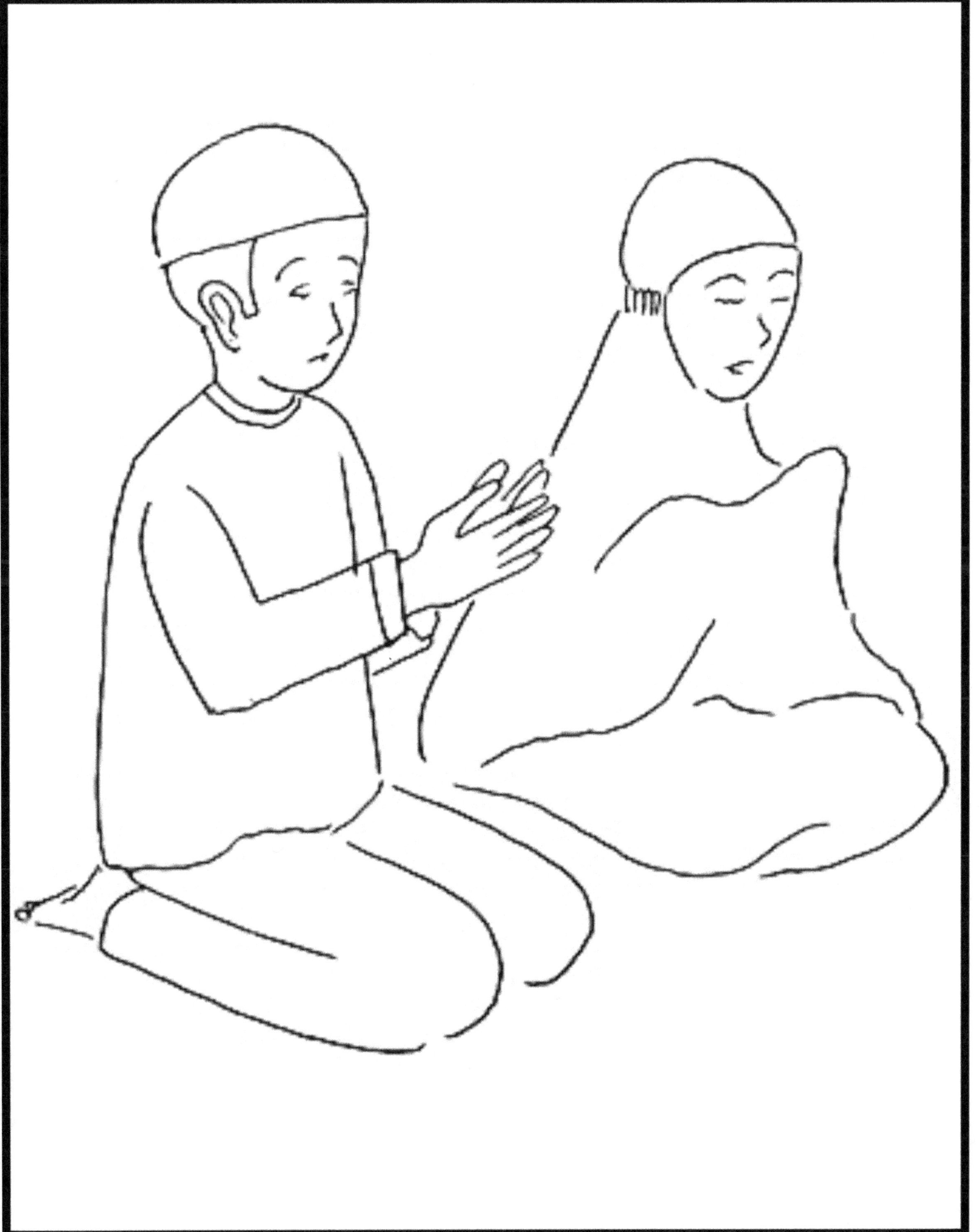

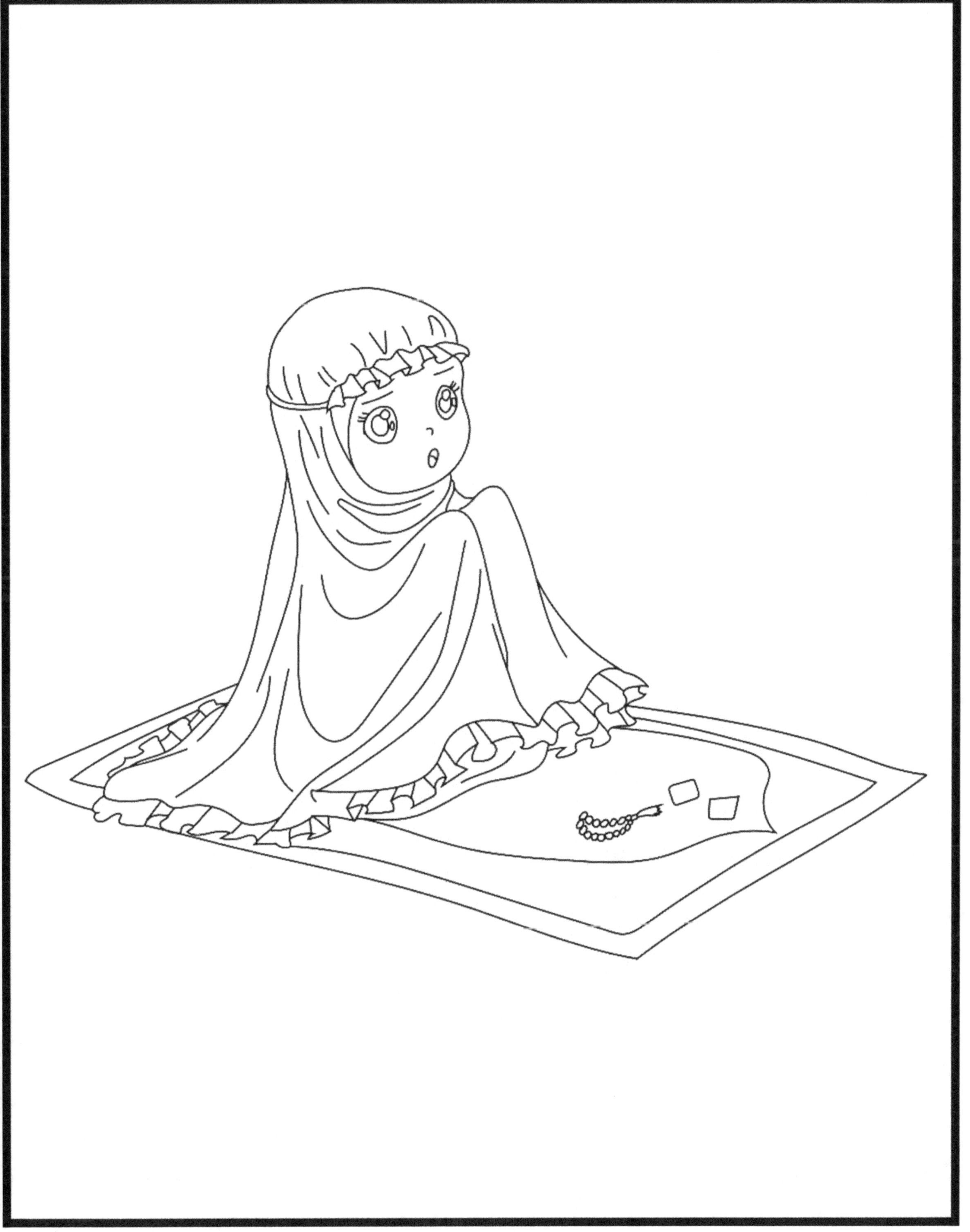

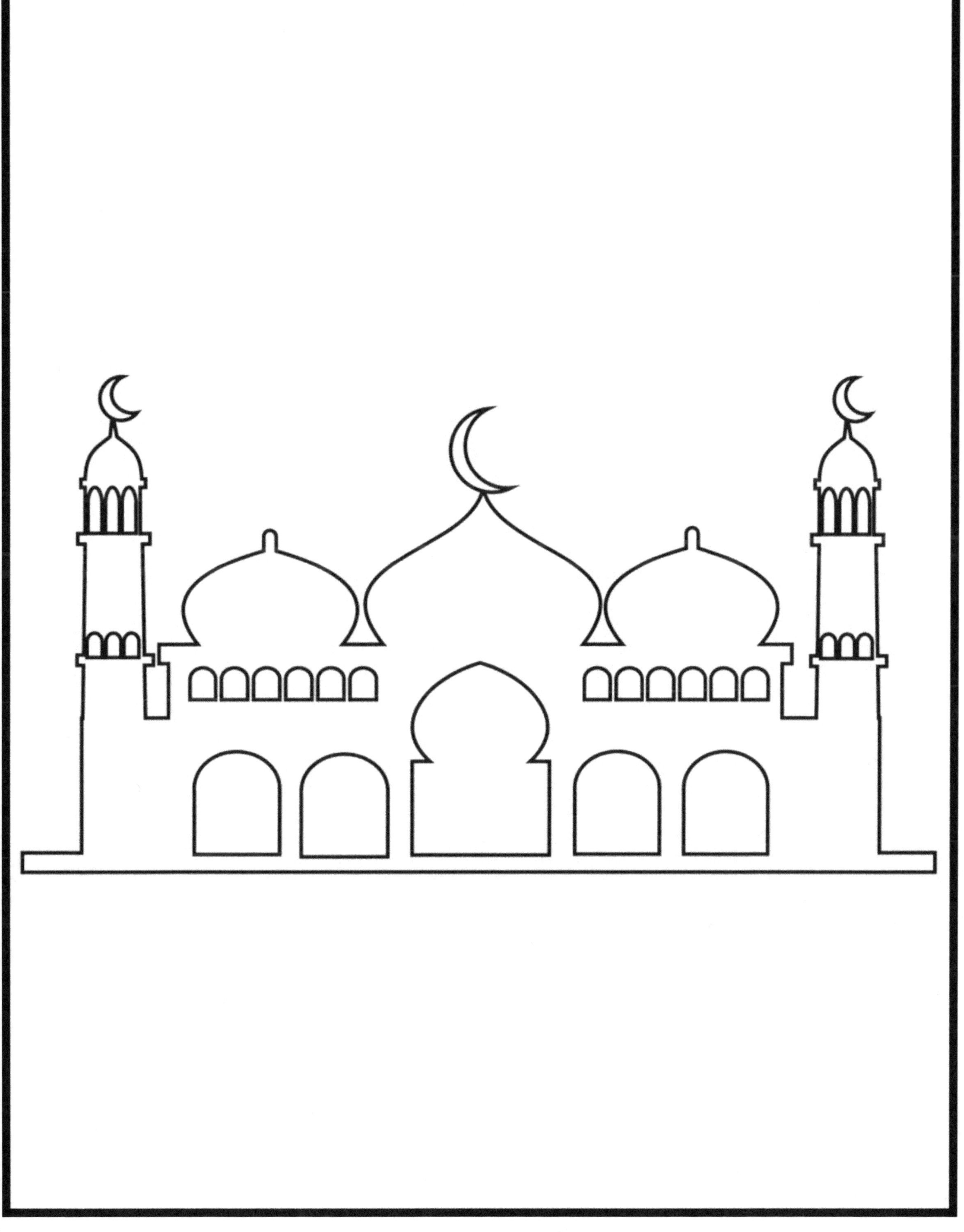

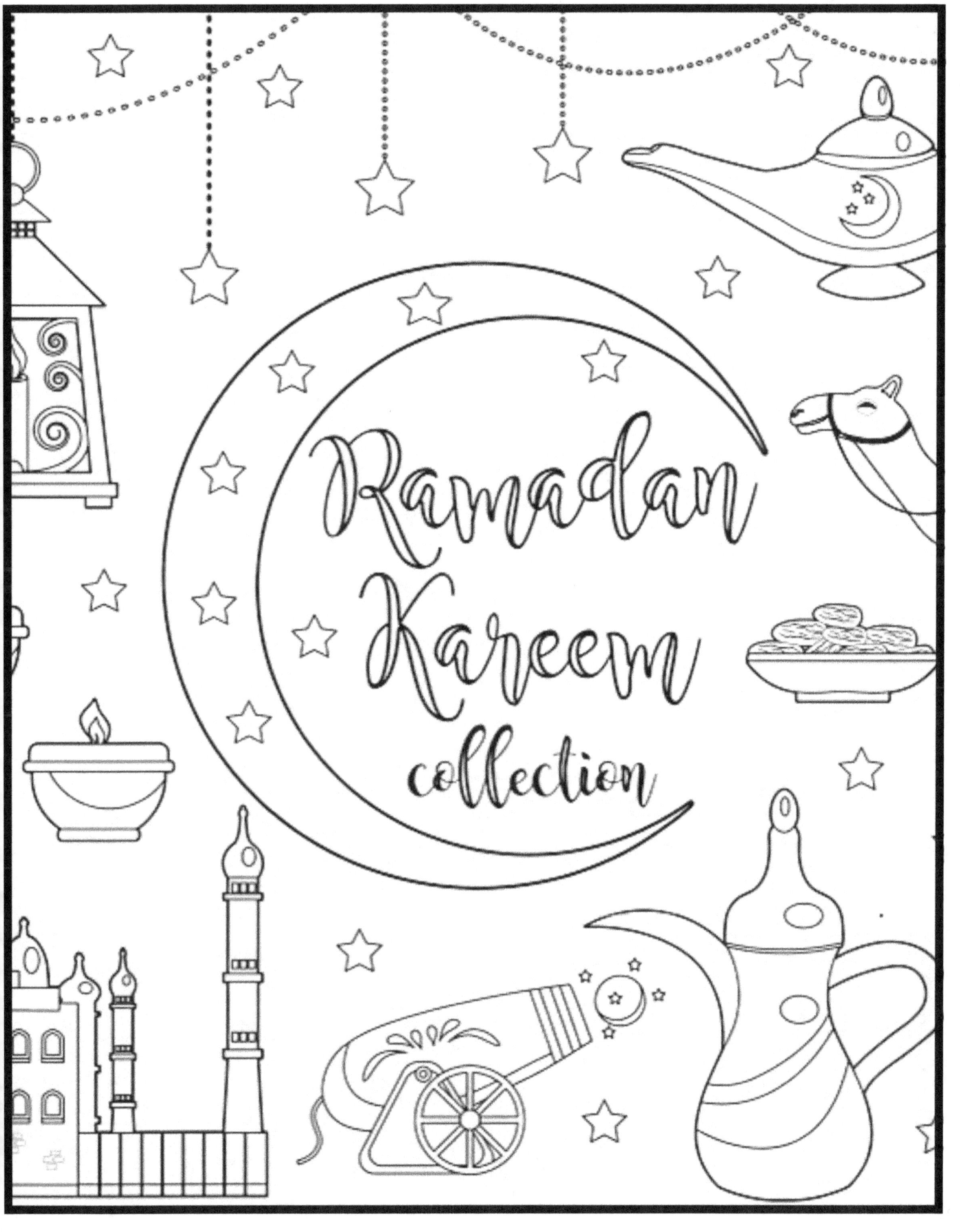

Ramadan
Kareem
collection

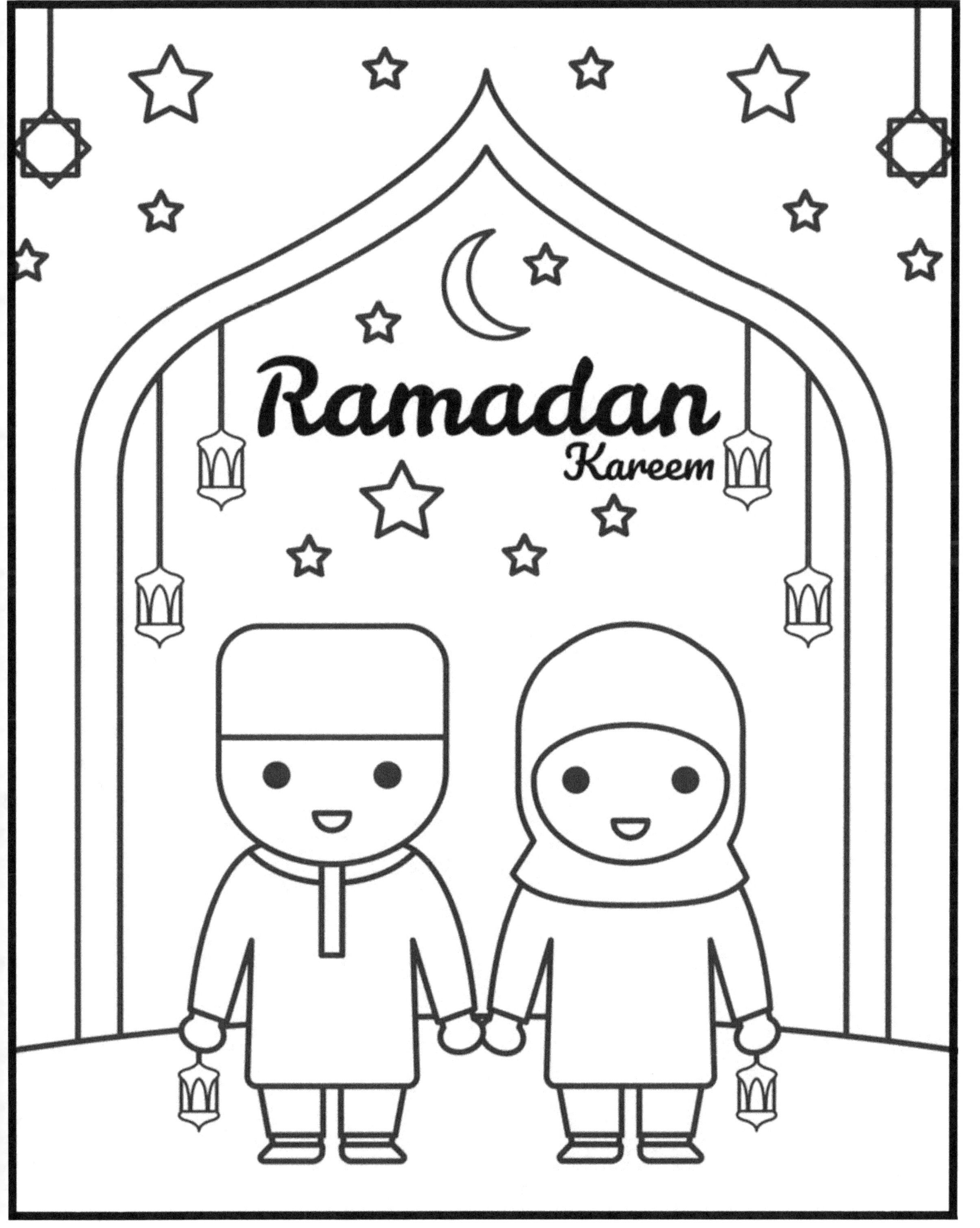

Ramadan
Kareem

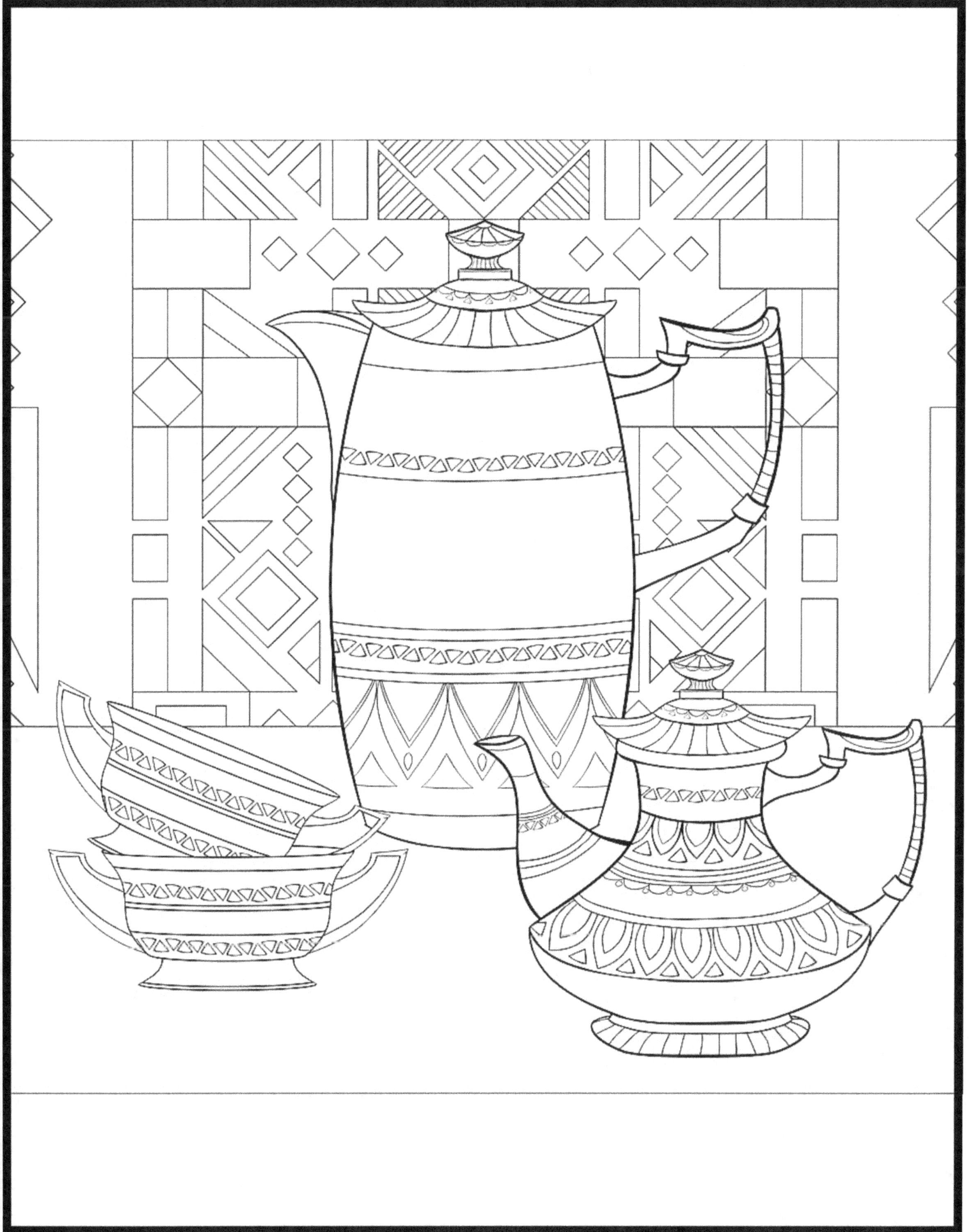

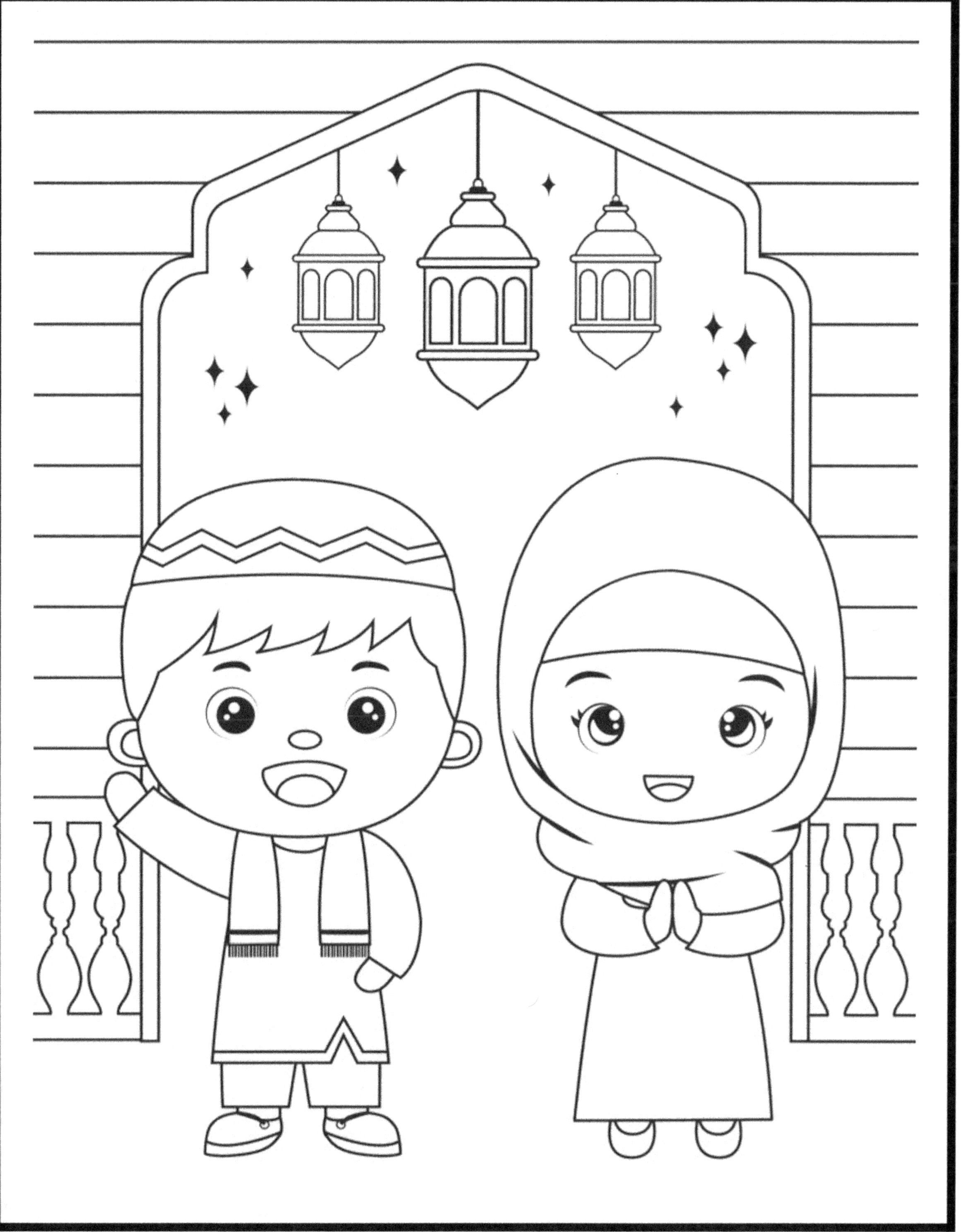

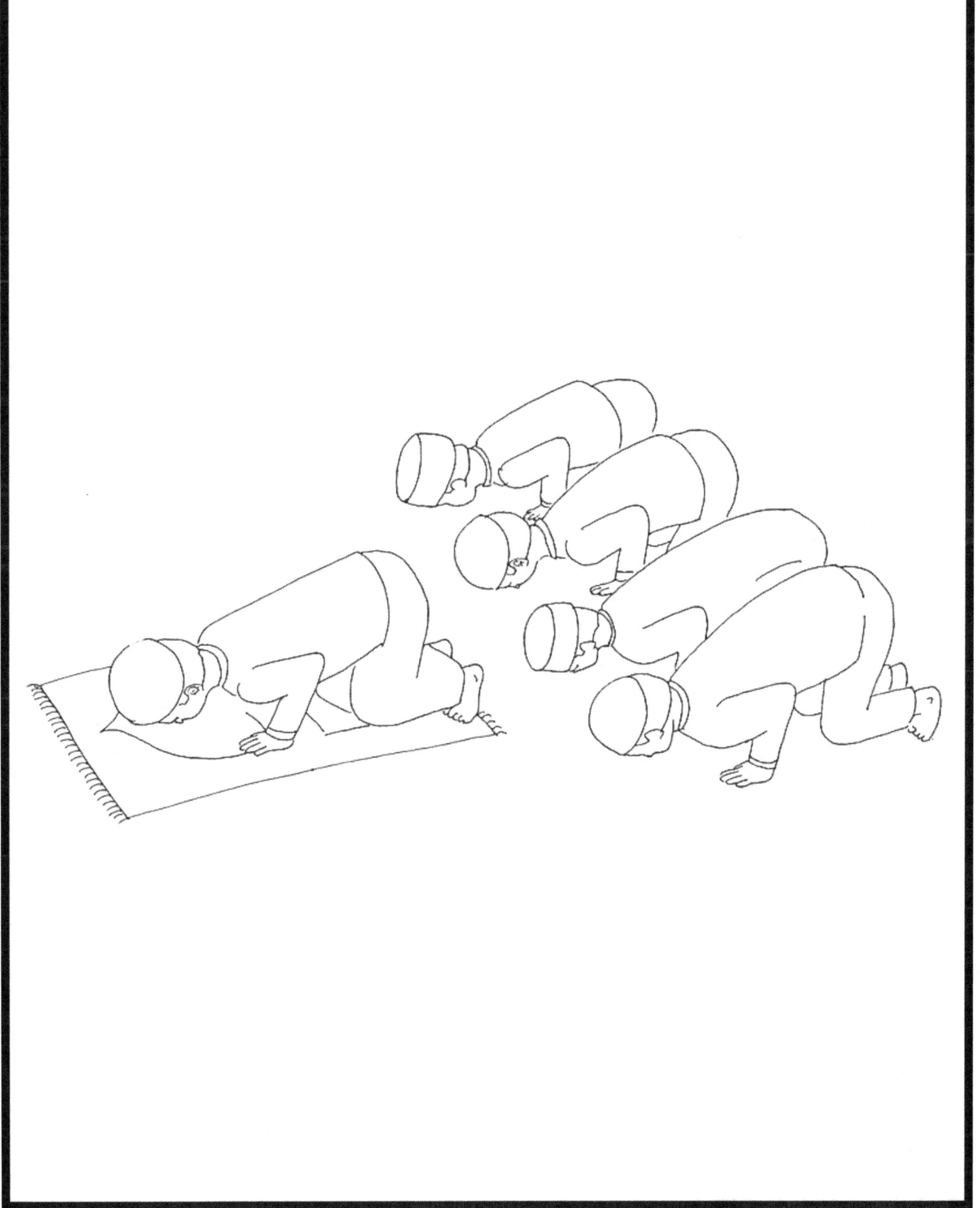

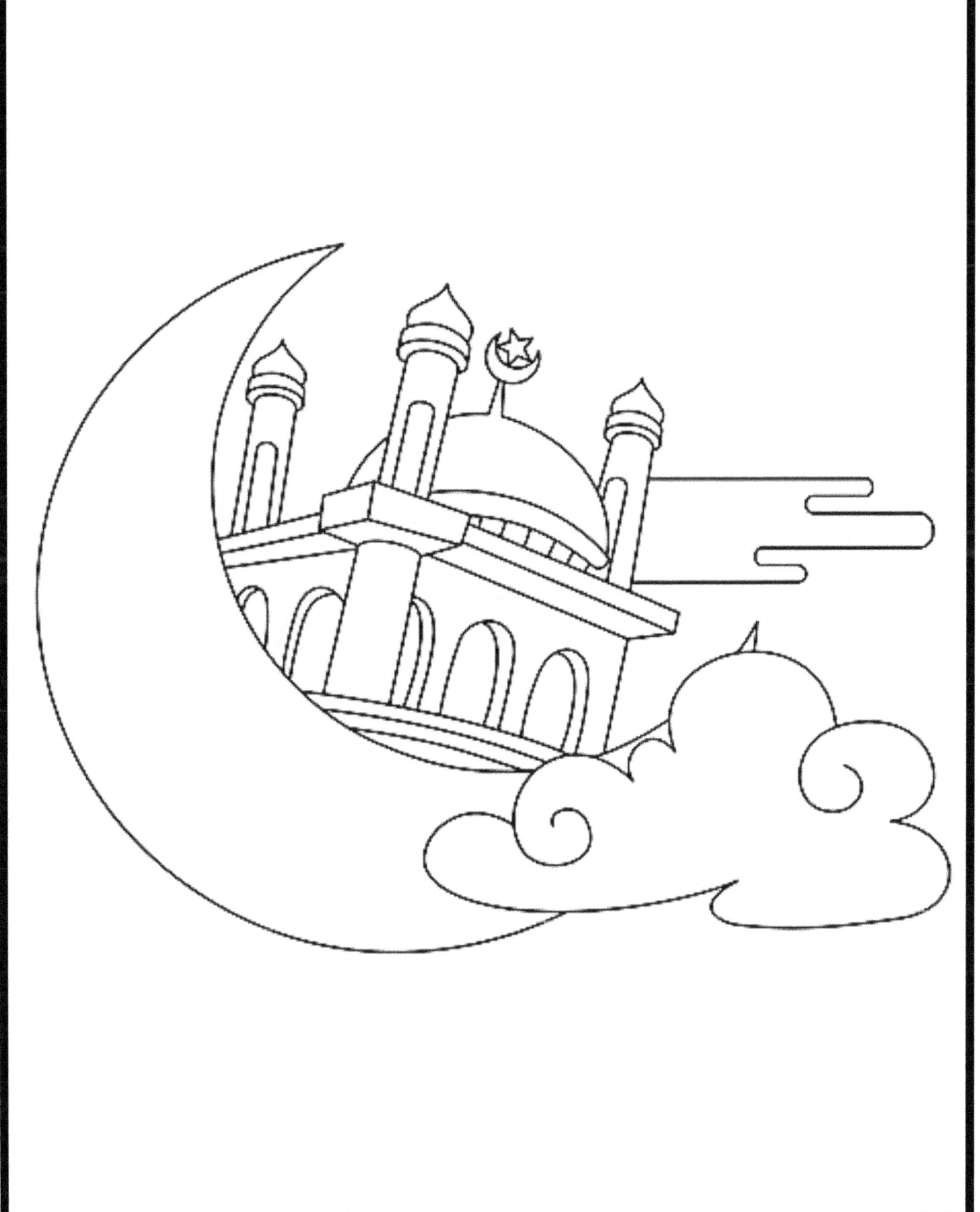

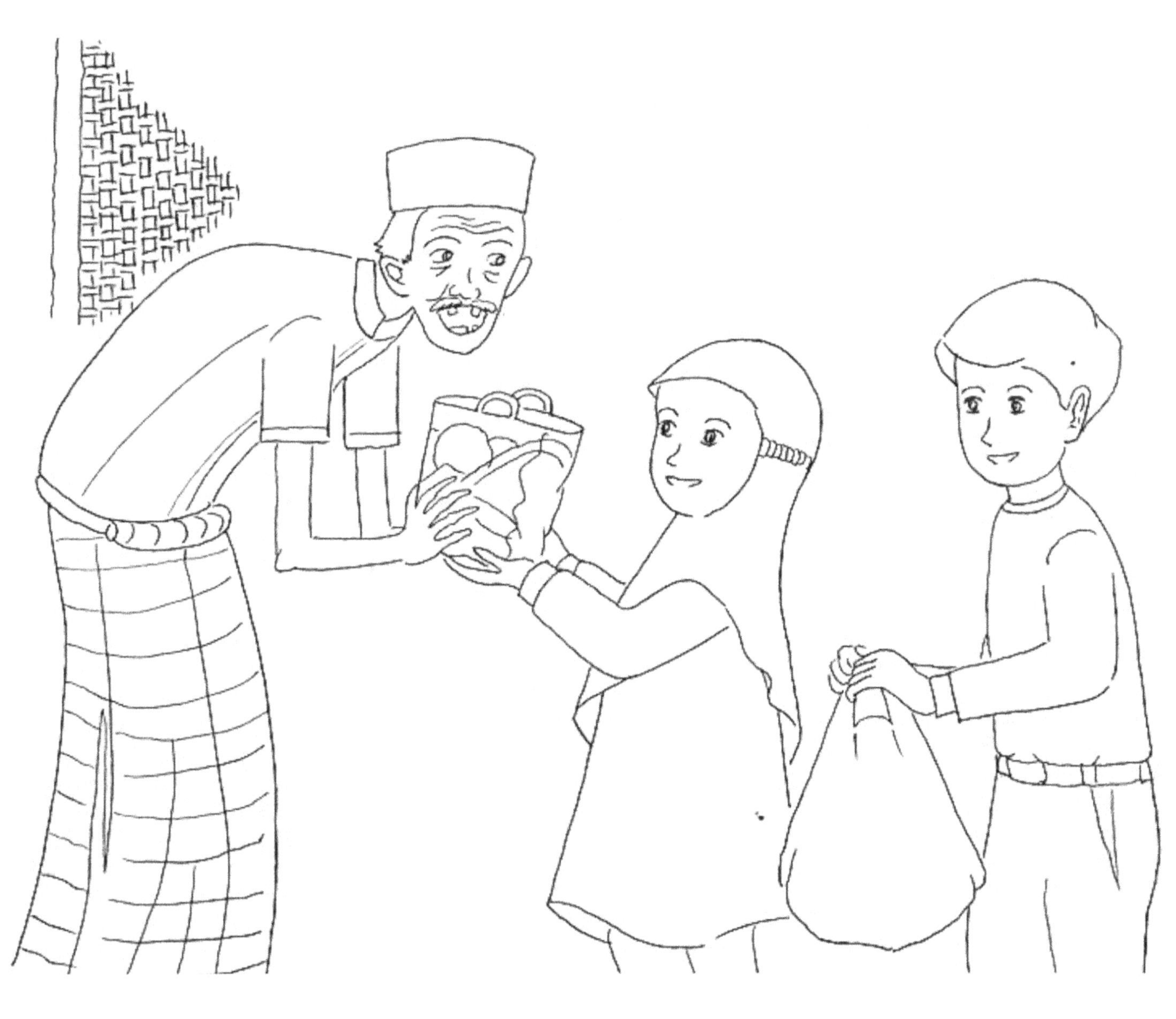

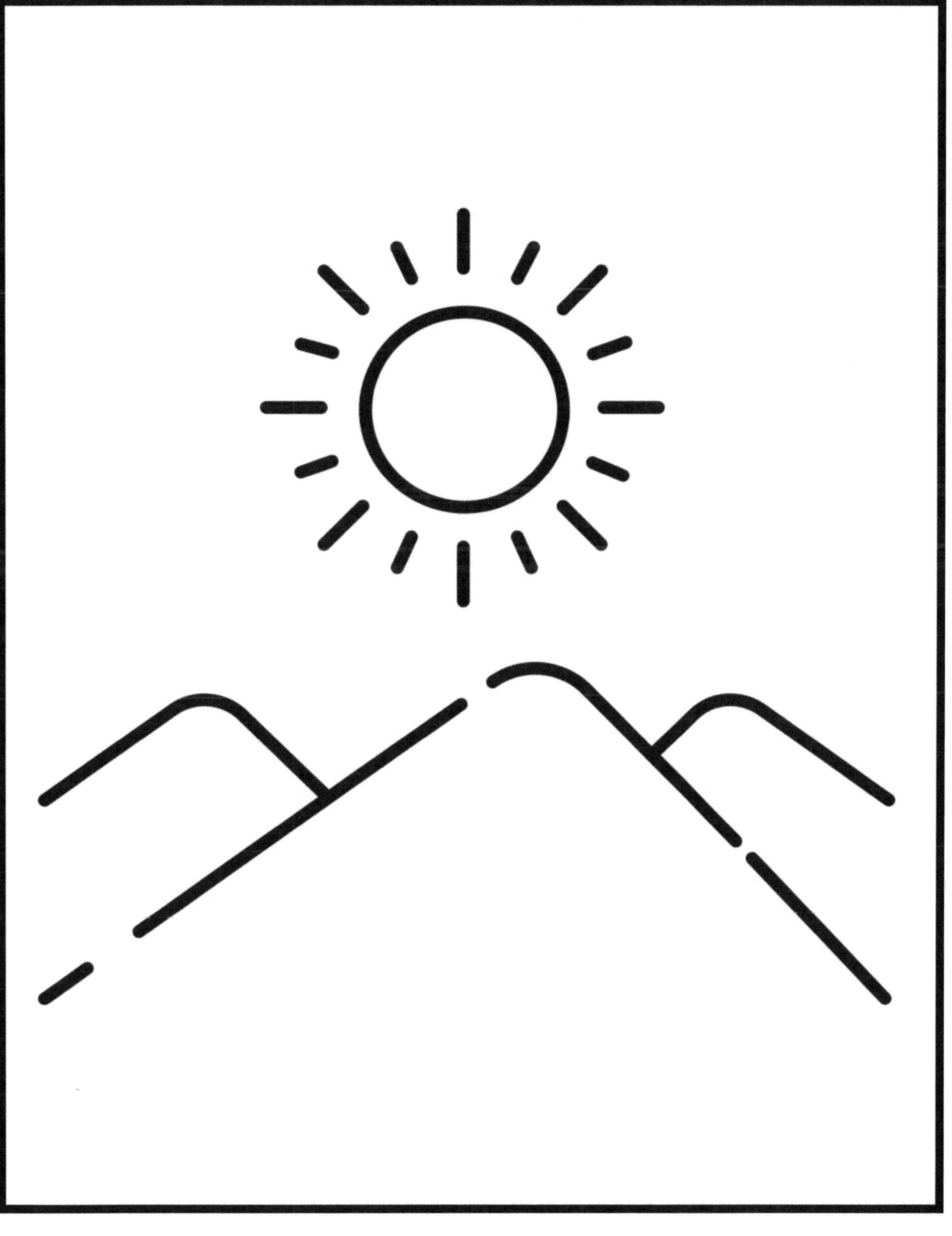

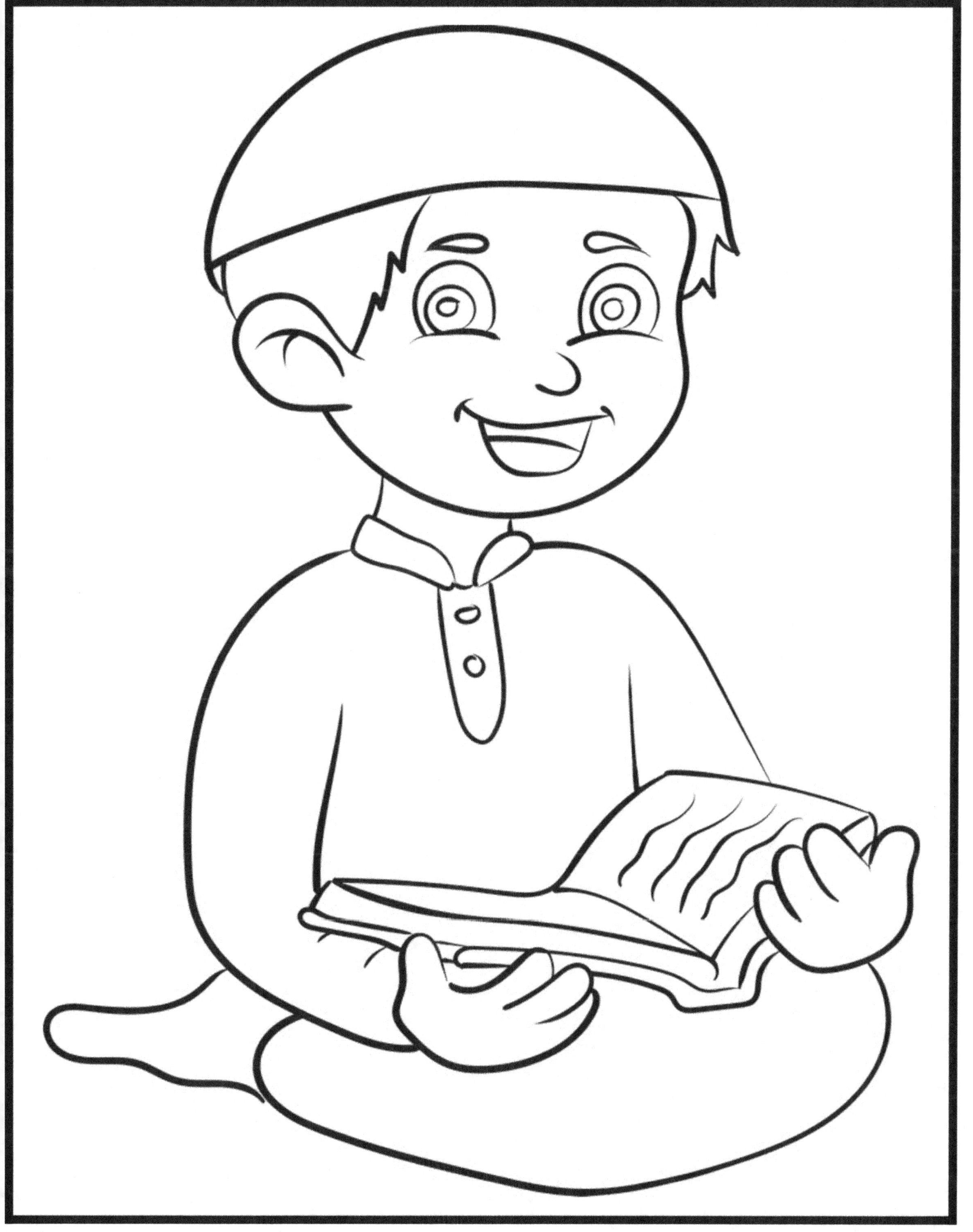

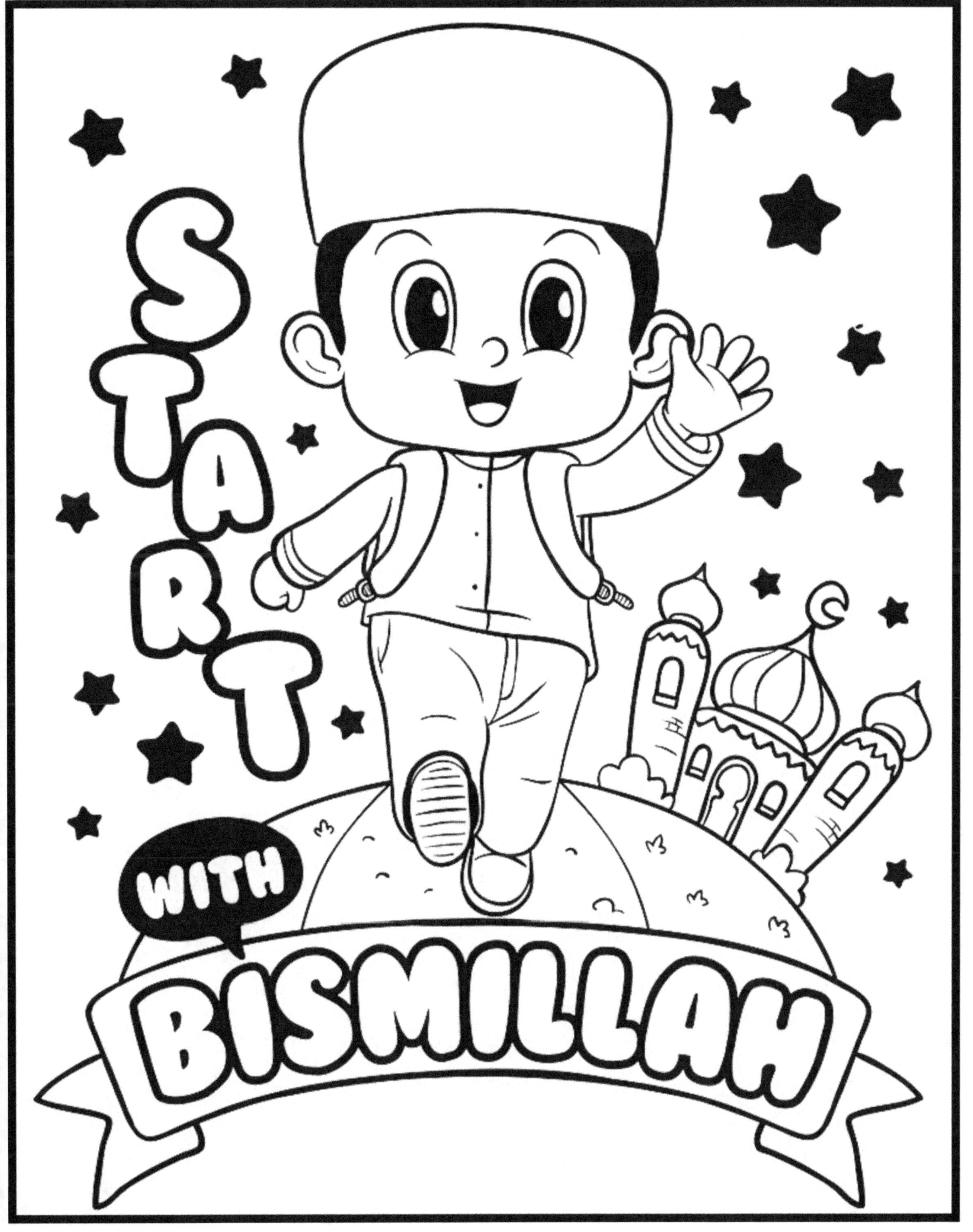

S
T
A
R
T
WITH
BISMILLAH

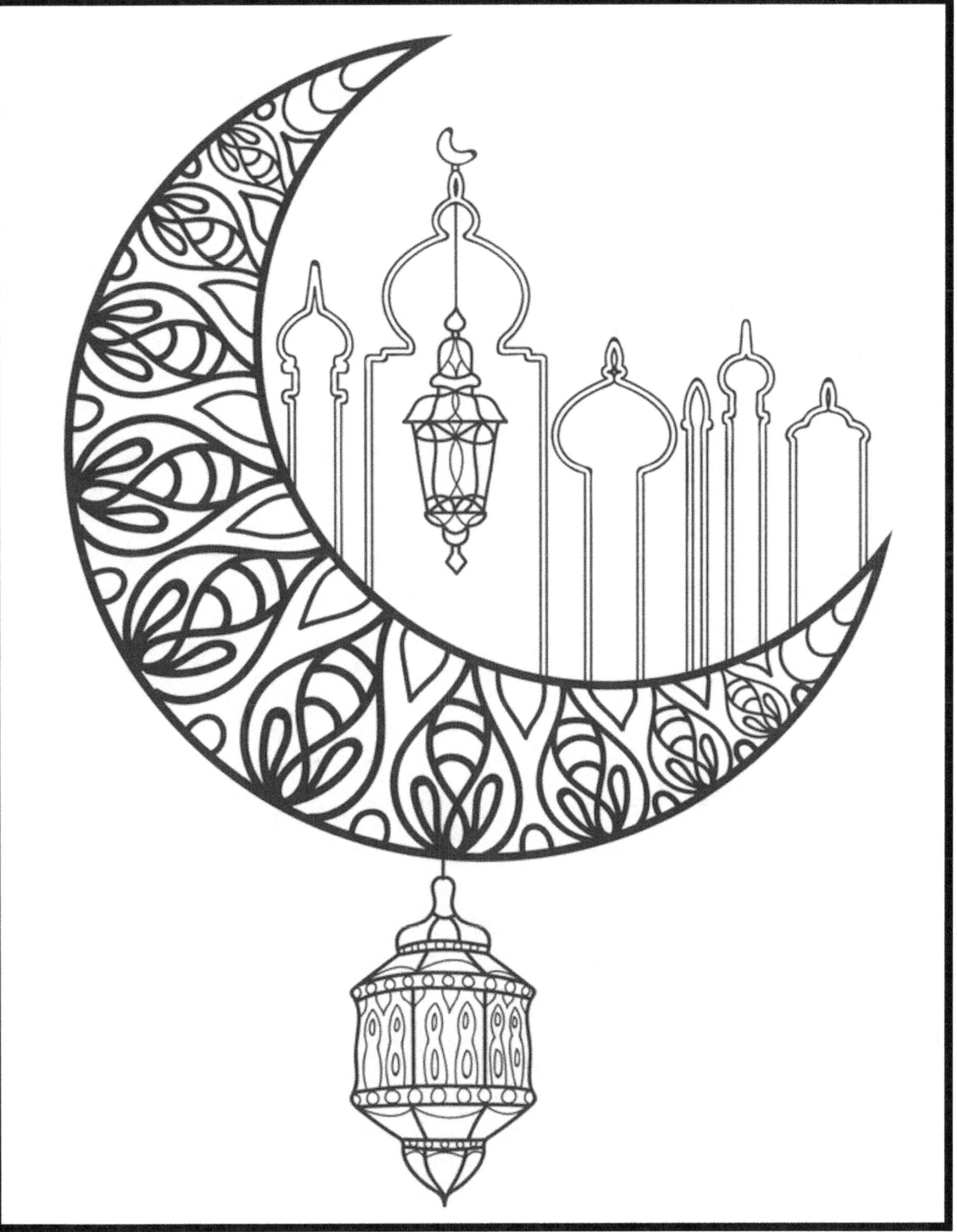

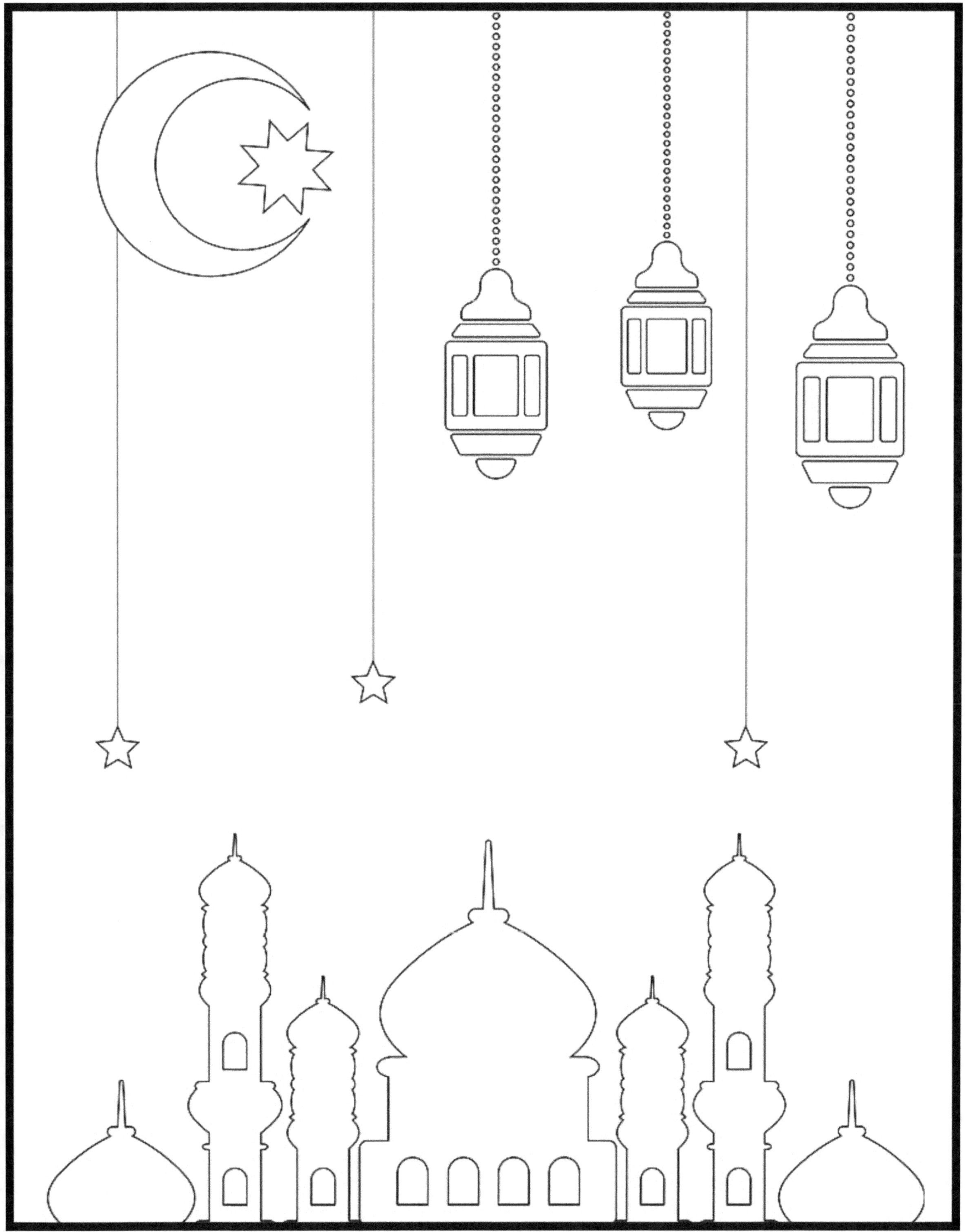

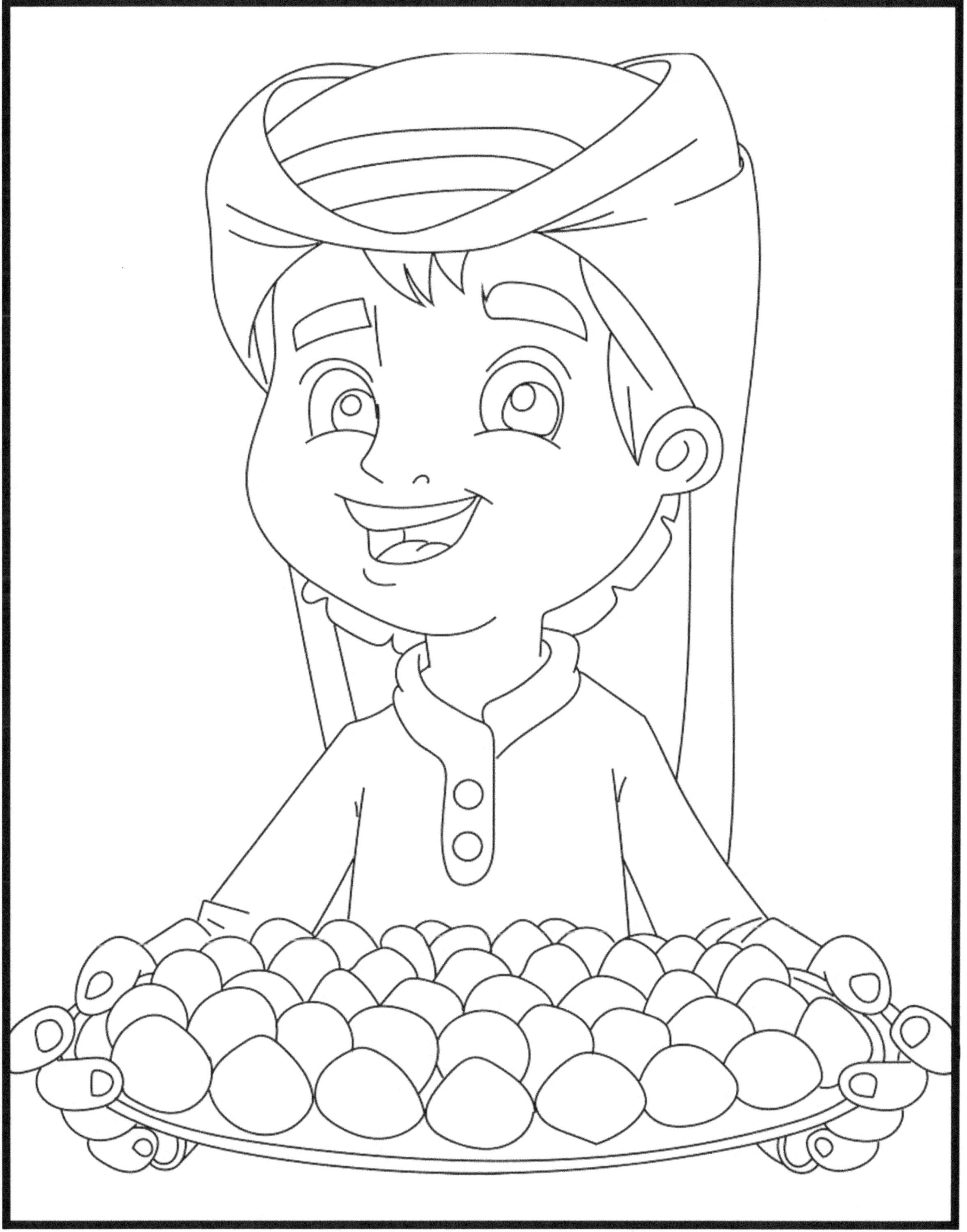

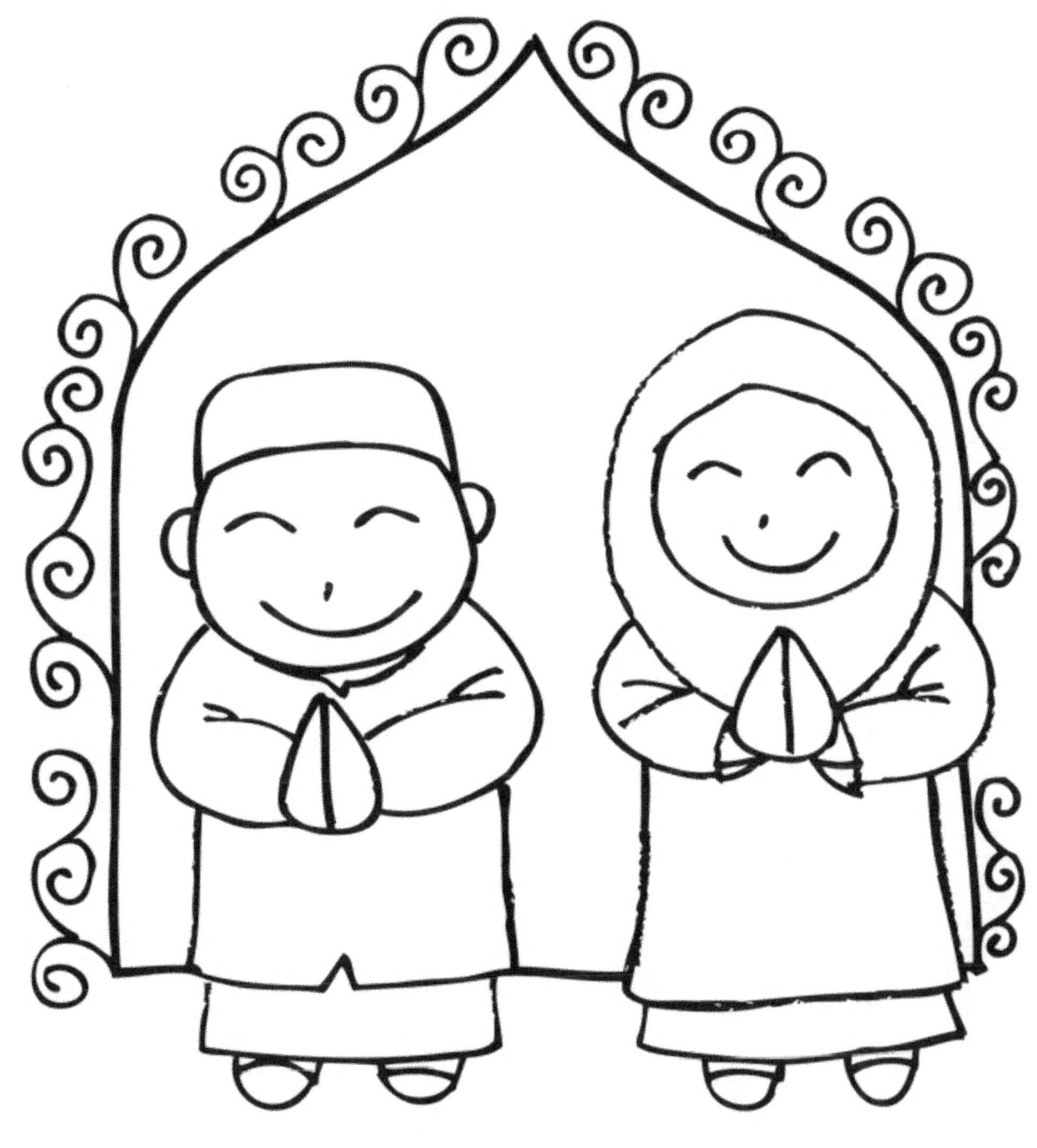

eid mubarak

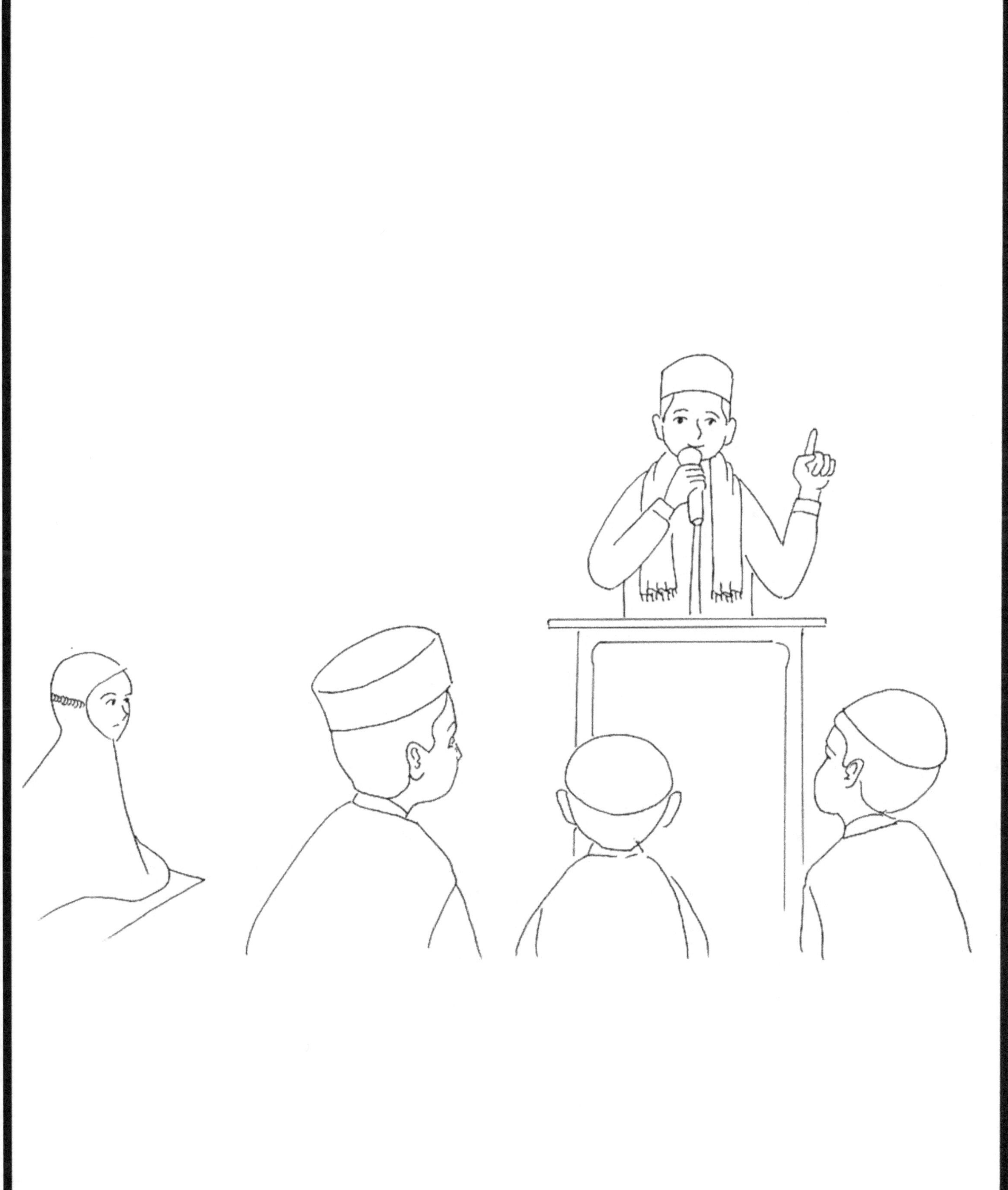

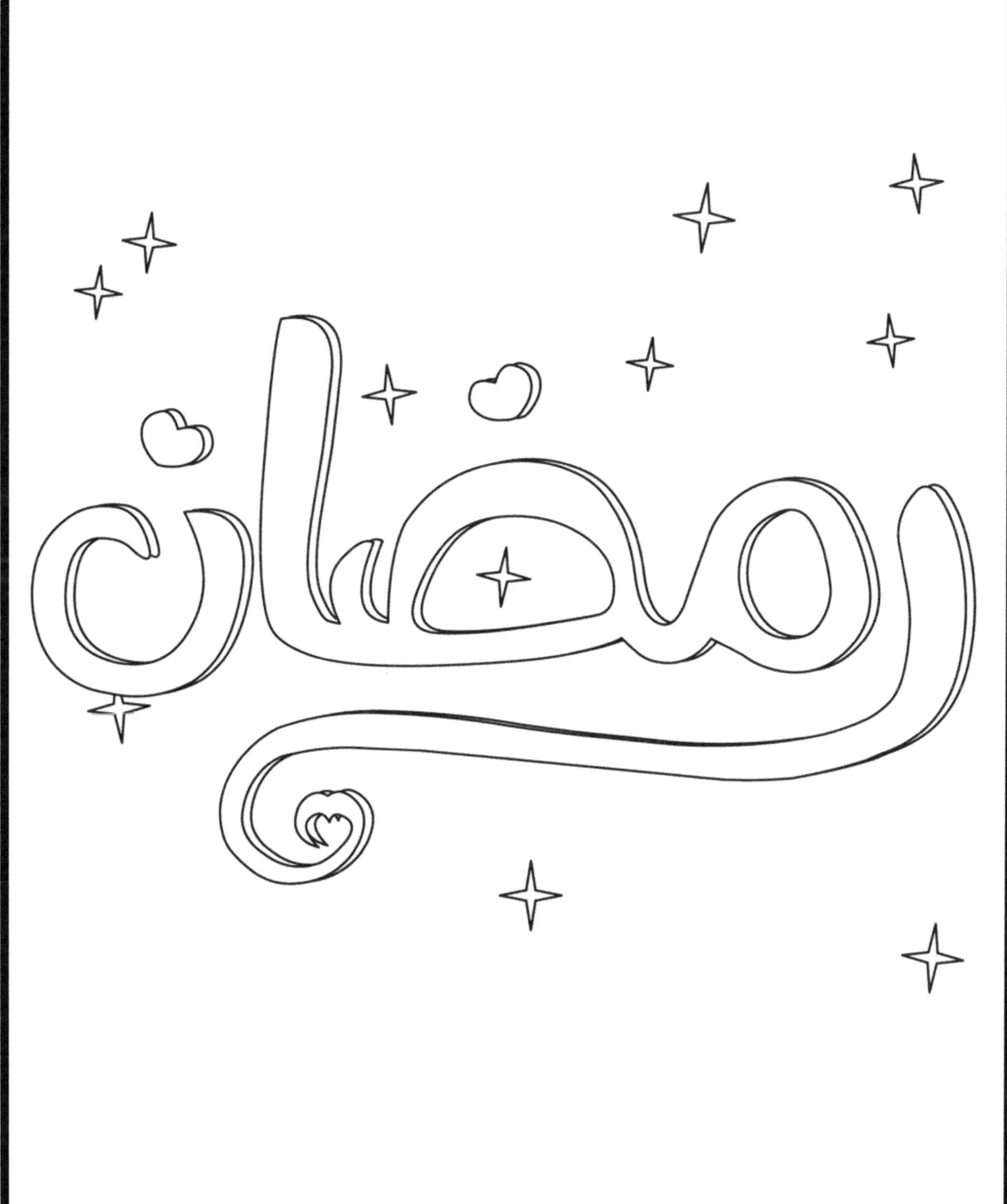

رمضان

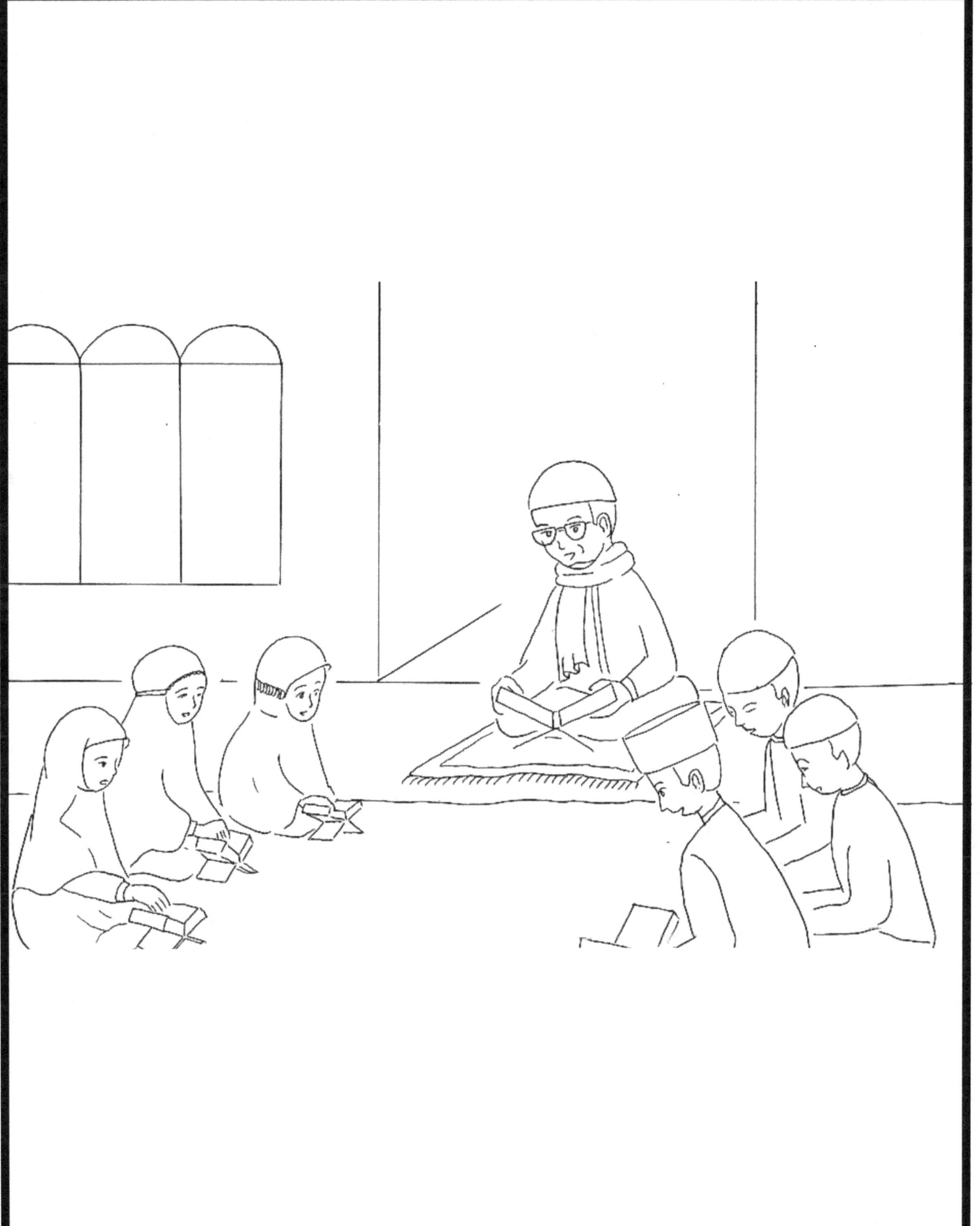

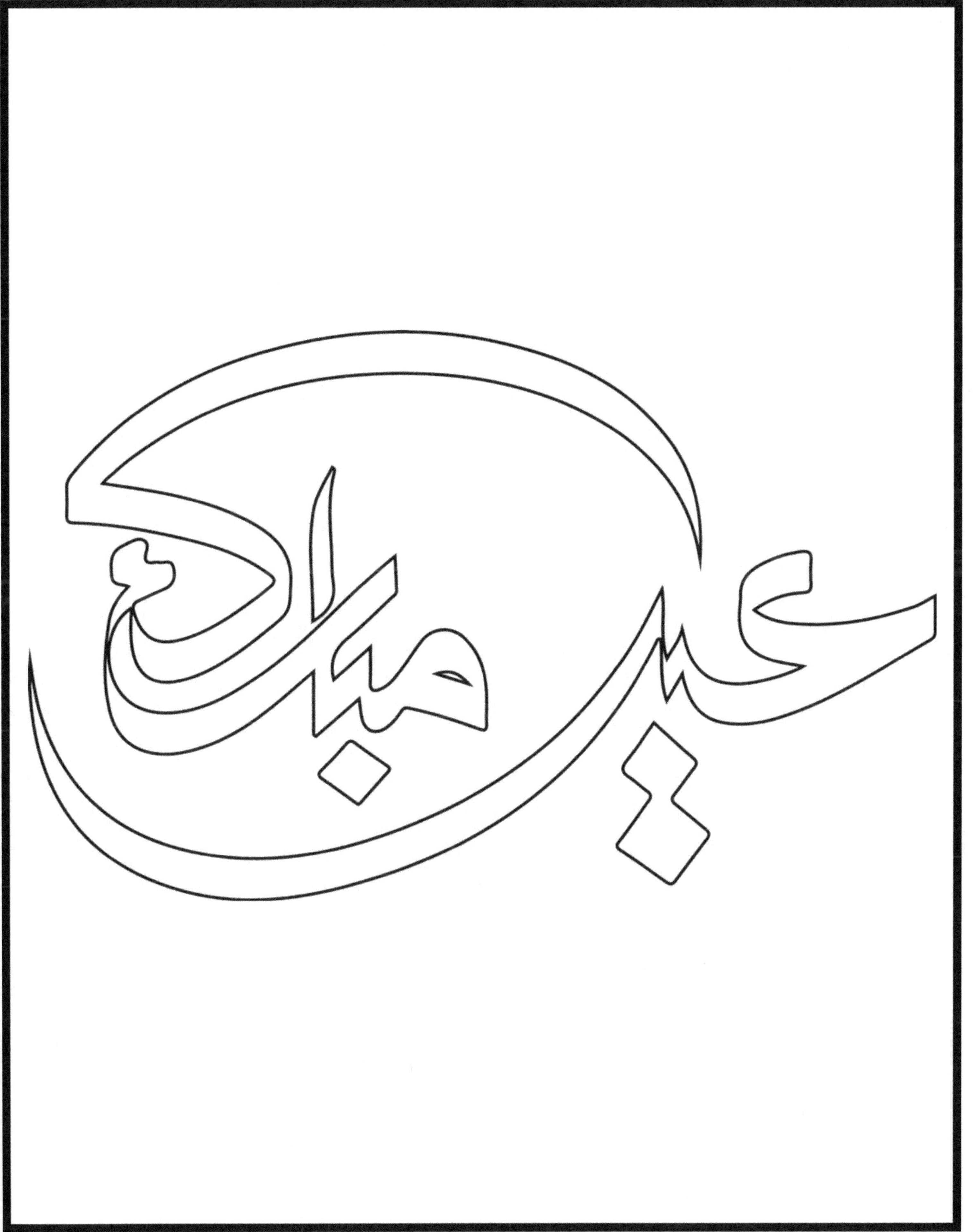
عيد مبارك

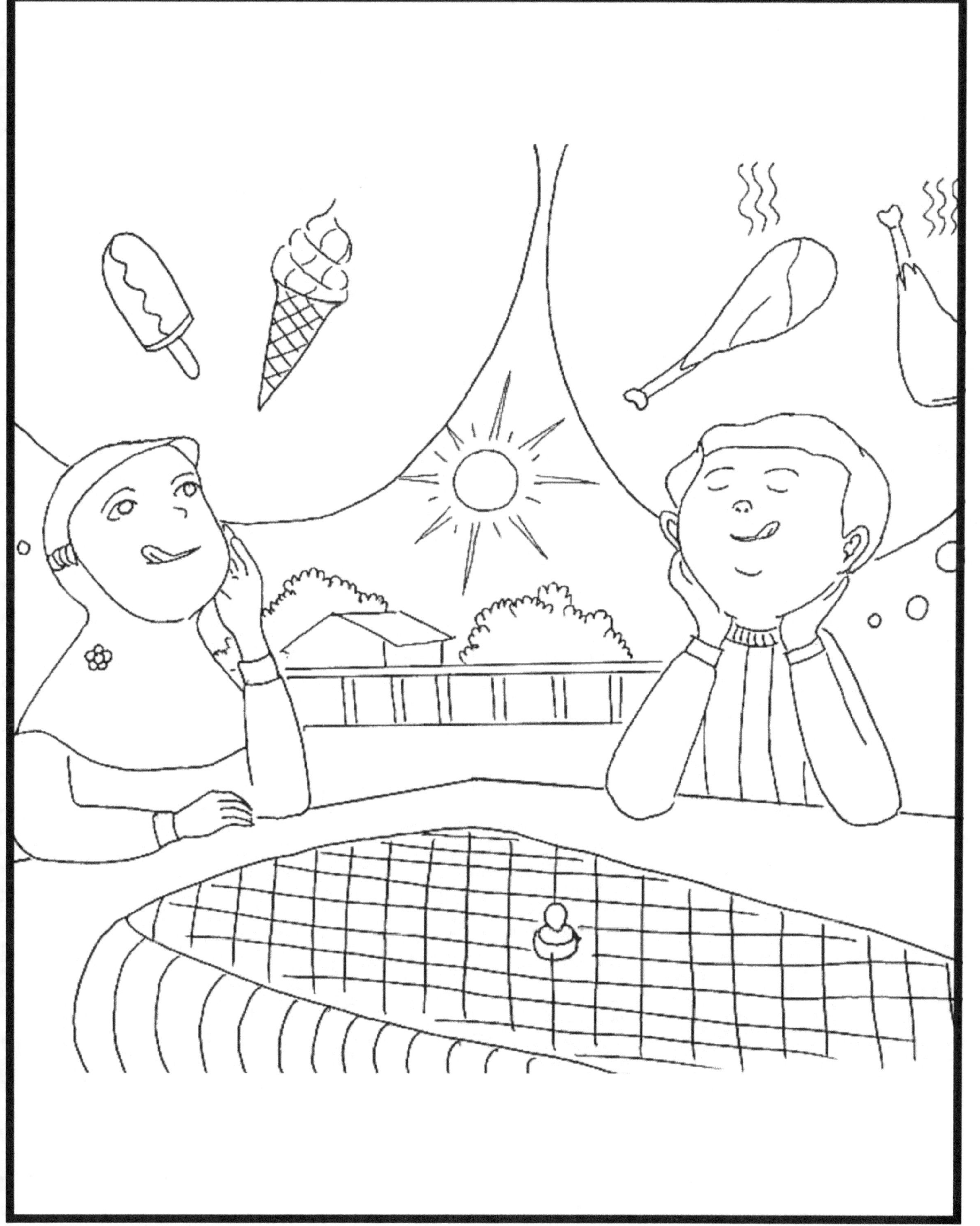

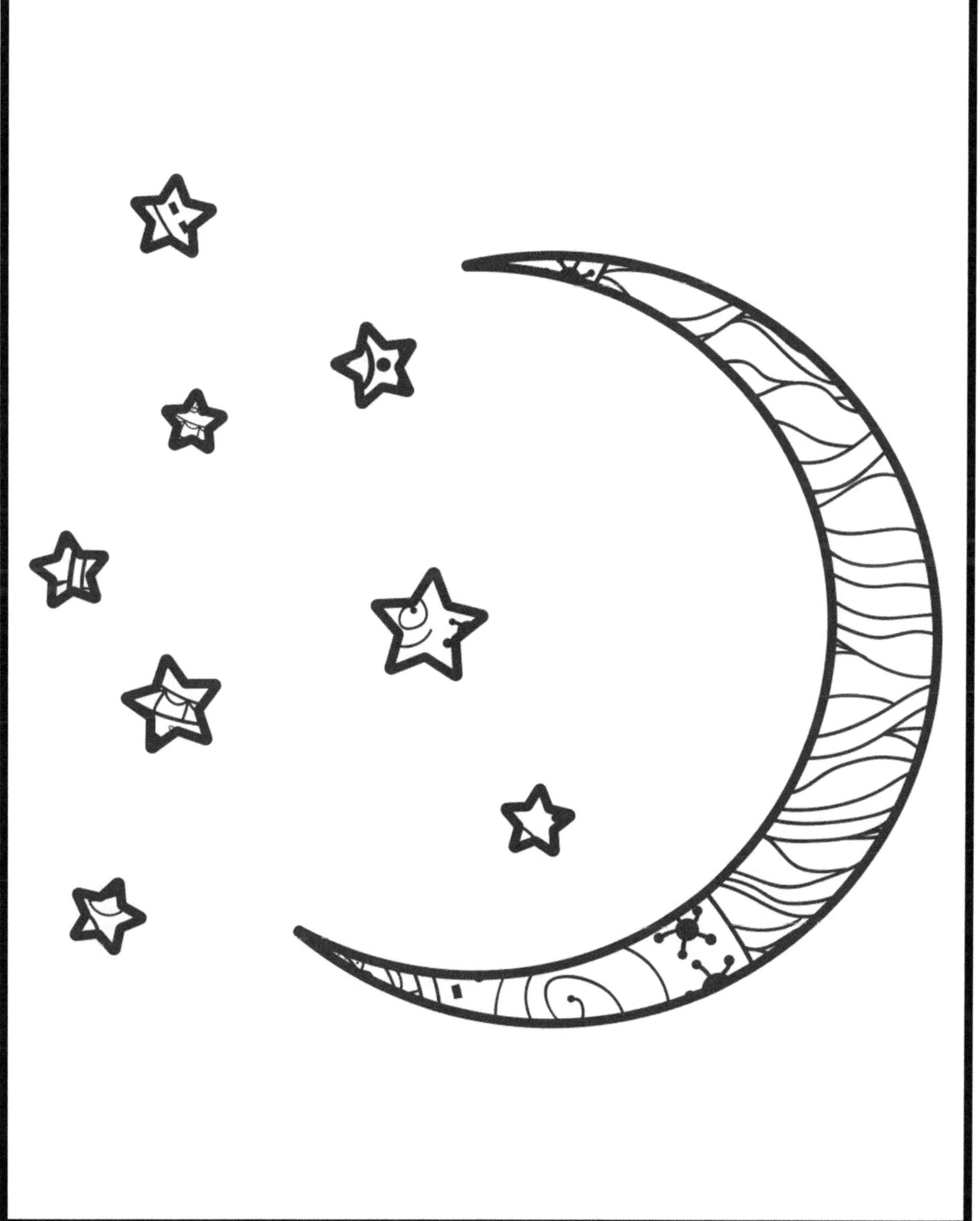

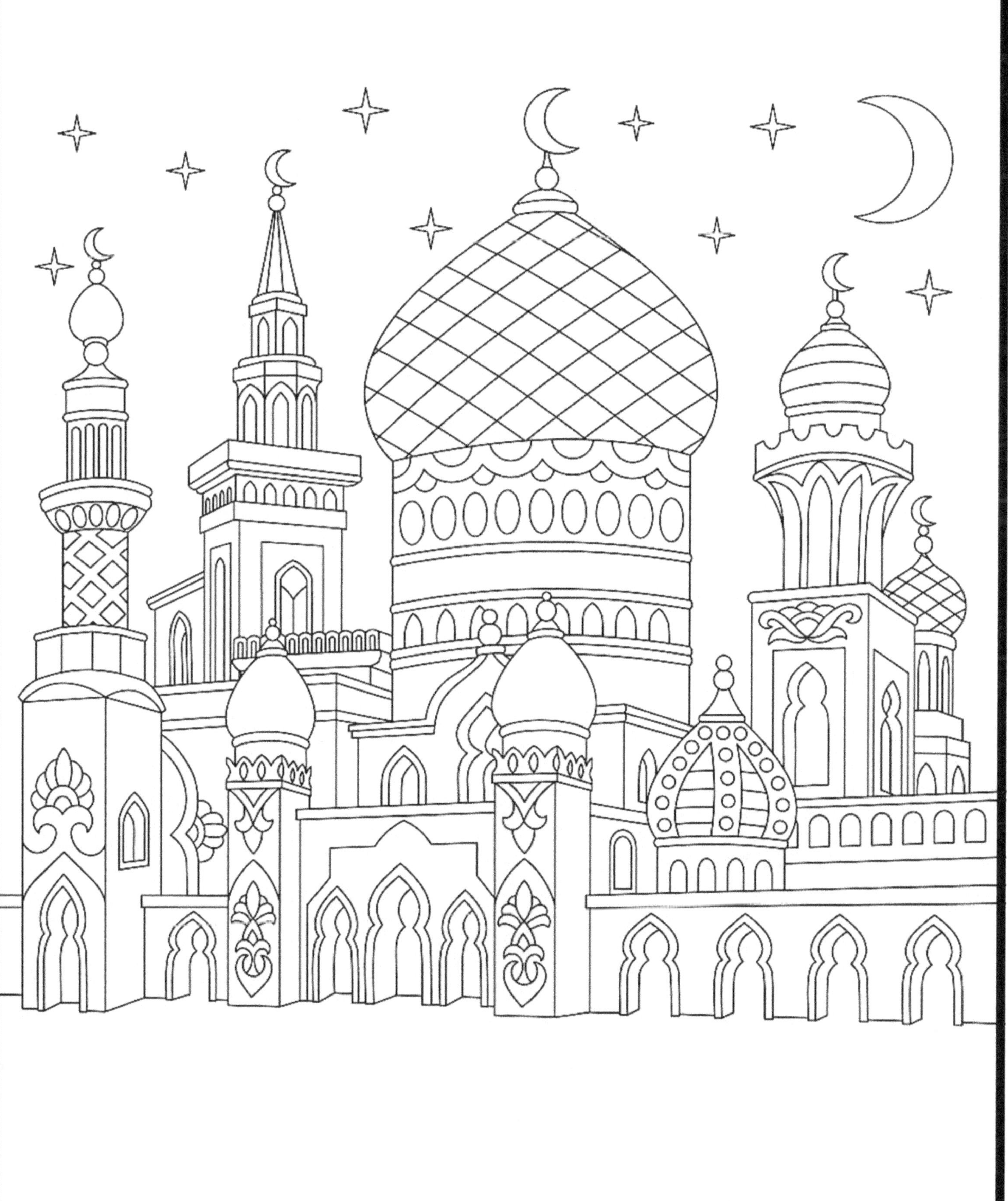